National Treasures

CONTENTS

NATIONAL GEOGRAPHIC School Publishing
Hampton-Brown

Syllables

Look at each picture. Read each word. How many syllables do you hear? How would you divide each word into syllables?

High Frequency Words

- best
- bring
- color
- face
- fly
- lot
- man
- same
- tree
- white

Key Words

Look at the pictures. Read the sentences.

A Hiking Man

1. This **man** knows he must **bring** water on hikes.
2. He hikes in parks he knows **best**.
3. He sees a **lot** of deer that are the **same color**.
4. He sees a bald eagle **fly** to a **tree**.
5. It has a **white face** and head.
6. The man has a nice hike!

What place do you think is best for hiking?

Phonics Games

NGReach.com

Exploring Two U.S. National Parks

by Ruben Alonzo

The United States has a lot of national parks. Look at the map. It shows the location of Yellowstone National Park. The map also shows the location of Big Bend National Park. Find these two parks on the map.

Name of Park	Year	Some Sights to See
Yellowstone National Park	1872	hot springs, Old Faithful, lakes, animals
Big Bend National Park	1944	canyons, desert, cactuses, mountains, river

Look at the chart. It gives information about these two parks. Yellowstone National Park is the oldest national park in the United States. When was it established? How would you compare the age of these two national parks?

Yellowstone

More than 3,000,000 people visit Yellowstone National Park in some years. It may be the best-known park in the United States. Yellowstone has many miles of roads. People can drive through the park to enjoy the sights.

Yellowstone National Park has more than 1,000 miles of trails. People can hike along these paths. They can enjoy nature. They can look at rivers and waterfalls, such as this one.

Old Faithful is a well-known feature at Yellowstone. It is a geyser that shoots hot water and steam up into the air every so often. The park has more than 200 geysers, but no one can be sure when they will shoot steam and water. But Old Faithful keeps shooting every day.

Yellowstone is filled with forests and animals. The best-known creatures in the park are probably grizzly bears and gray wolves.

There were no wolves in Yellowstone for almost 70 years. A few dozen were turned loose in the park in 1995. Now there are over a hundred.

A lucky Yellowstone visitor may catch sight of this white face high up in a tree. It is a bald eagle. If you are lucky enough to see one, stay still and silent. Don't startle the bird, or it will fly off.

cactus

Big Bend

Much of Big Bend National Park is desert. A smart hiker, like the man in this picture, brings water in a backpack when hiking its trails.

People often visit in spring. The cactuses are in bloom then. A cactus is a plant. Many cactuses have spines, or thorns. Can you find the spines?

Big Bend National Park has mountains. Visitors can go hiking. They should be careful. Mountain lions roam the park! Can you find the mountain lion? Its color helps it to blend in with the landscape.

A river forms part of the border of Big Bend National Park. The river is the Rio Grande. It has carved deep canyons into the ground. This amazing canyon has walls that reach up 1500 feet.

These two parks are different in some ways. Yellowstone has geysers and forests. Big Bend has deserts and cactuses.

But these parks are the same in many ways. Both have hiking trails, wild animals, and amazing sights to see!

Syllables

Read these words.

landscape	enjoy	roam	amazing	visit
attractions	park	canyon	nature	steam

Find the words with more than one syllable.
Use letters to build them.

l a n d s c a p e

Talk Together

Choose words from the box above to tell your partner what visitors can do in this place.

Syllable Division

Look at each picture. Read each word. How did you know where to divide it into syllables?

trumpet

eagle

High Frequency Words
best
bring
color
face
fly
lot
man
same
tree
white

Key Words

Look at the pictures. Read the sentences.

U.S. Symbols

1. Uncle Sam is one of the **best**-known U.S. symbols.
2. He is a **man** with a **lot** of **white** hair on his **face**.
3. The bald eagle's head is that **same** **color**.
4. This bald eagle is about to **fly** from the **tree**.
5. A ship had to **bring** this statue to America.

Phonics Games

NGReach.com

Exploring National Symbols

by Carmen Flores

U.S. Flag

This flag is a symbol of the United States. It has fifty stars. Each star stands for one of the fifty states. The thirteen stripes stand for the thirteen states that first formed our nation, back in 1776.

In 1777, a group of people agreed that the flag should have thirteen stripes and thirteen stars. No one wrote instructions about arranging the stars. So some flags from that time have the stars in rows. Other flags have the stars in a circle. How are the stars arranged on this flag?

Bald Eagle

Another major U.S. symbol is the bald eagle, the national bird of the United States. Do the bald eagles in this tree look bald to you? Their heads are not bare, of course. Those are white feathers growing on their heads, necks, and faces.

The bald eagle lives only in North America. It is a big, powerful bird. Look at it spread its wings and fly! Why is the bald eagle an excellent symbol for the United States?

The Great Seal

This same bird is on the front of the Great Seal, another U.S. symbol. The eagle holds arrows in one claw, to show that the United States is ready to fight. But it also holds an olive branch for peace.

The Oak Tree

Did you know that the oak is the national tree of the United States? This tree is hardy and lives a long time. It has strong wood. Why is the oak tree a good symbol of the United States?

Uncle Sam

Look at the picture of Uncle Sam. He may be one of the best-known symbols of the United States. Uncle Sam is not a real man. Artists drew Uncle Sam in cartoons and in posters.

Uncle Sam is tall and thin. He has a white beard on his face. His hair is the same color, too. Uncle Sam wears a top hat. His clothes are often red, white, and blue. He may be wearing stars and stripes. Which of the men in this cartoon is Uncle Sam?

The Statue of Liberty

This huge statue is another symbol of the United States. It was a gift from the people of France to the people of the United States. The statue stands for liberty and being free.

The Statue of Liberty is huge. Artists made the statue in France. Then workers took it apart. A ship had to bring the parts to New York. The ship arrived in New York in 1885. Then workers reconnected the parts of the statue.

More U.S. symbols include the White House and the song "Yankee Doddle Dandy." The rose is the national flower. The national march is "The Stars and Stripes Forever."

Which symbol do you think of when you think of the United States?

Syllable Division

Read these words.

lady	locate	bird	symbol
eagle	visit	united	statue

Find the words with more than one syllable.
Use letters to build them.

e a g l e

Talk Together

Choose words from the box above to tell your partner about the symbol in each picture.

The eagle is a symbol.

Find the Amazing Sights

Find the sights to see in the park. Look at the picture with a partner. Take turns reading the items and pointing to answers. Find these things:

1. a bald eagle in a tree
2. a man holding a fishnet with a fish
3. two baby animals of the same color
4. a creature with a white face and body
5. a lot of deer grazing around a lake
6. one adult mountain lion that is partly hidden

Acknowledgments
Grateful acknowledgment is given to the authors, artists, photographers, museums, publishers, and agents for permission to reprint copyrighted material. Every effort has been made to secure the appropriate permission. If any omissions have been made or if corrections are required, please contact the Publisher.

Photographic Credits
CVR Al Bello/Getty Images. **2** (b) Corbis/Photolibrary. (t) Jose Luis Pelaez, Inc./Blend Images/Corbis. **3** (b) Liz Garza Williams/Hampton-Brown/National Geographic School Publishing. (tc) Philippe Clement/Nature Picture Library. (tl) Nick Daly/Getty Images. (tr) Winfield Parks/National Geographic Image Collection. **4** (l) NPS Photo by Jim Peaco/National Park Service. (tr) Andre Jenny/Alamy Images. **4-5** (c) Skip O'Donnell/iStockphoto. 5 (bg) Brandon Laufenberg/iStockphoto. **6-7** (c) Skip O'Donnell/iStockphoto. (tl) Rob Crandall/ Alamy Images. **7** (bg) Brandon Laufenberg/iStockphoto. (t) Ron Niebrugge/Alamy Images. **8** JTB Photo Communications, Inc./Alamy Images. **8-9** (c) Skip O'Donnell/iStockphoto. **9** (bg) Brandon Laufenberg/iStockphoto. (cr) D Robert Franz/Photoshot. (tl) Jeff Vanuga/Corbis. **10** Stockbyte/Getty Images. **10-11** (c) Skip O'Donnell/iStockphoto. **11** (bg) Brandon Laufenberg/ iStockphoto. (c) Rob Howard/Terra/Corbis. (t) David Muench/Corbis. **12-13** (c) Skip O'Donnell/ iStockphoto. (tl) Dr. Maurice G. Hornocker/National Geographic Image Collection. **13** (bg) Brandon Laufenberg/iStockphoto. (t) David Muench/Corbis. **14** (bg) Brandon Laufenberg/ iStockphoto. (c) Skip O'Donnell/iStockphoto. (cr) Lisa Kyle Young/iStockphoto. (tl) Conor Quinlan/iStockphoto. **15** (b) Glenn Randall. (cr) Liz Garza Williams/Hampton-Brown/National Geographic School Publishing. **16** (b) Thomas Northcut/Getty Images. (c) Dave Bradley Photography/Getty Images. (tl) Artville. (tr) Martin Lukasiewicz/National Geographic Image Collection. **17** (b) Liz Garza Williams/Hampton-Brown/National Geographic School Publishing. (tc) Michael S. Quinton/National Geographic Image Collection. (tr) MISHELLA/Shutterstock. (tr) Larry Mulvehill/The Image Works, Inc. **18** david sanger photography/Alamy Images. **19** (bg) Angela Cable/iStockphoto. (t) Lee Snider/Photo Images/Corbis. **20** (bg) Angela Cable/ iStockphoto. (t) Alaska Stock Images/National Geographic Image Collection. **20-21** (tr) Jason Watson/Shutterstock. **22** (bg) Angela Cable/iStockphoto. (t) Andrew B. Graham/Getty Images. **22-23** (tr) Stephen St. John/National Geographic Image Collection. **24** (t) Prints & Photographs Division, Library of Congress, LC-USZC4-3859. **24-25** (bg) Angela Cable/iStockphoto. **25** (t) Prints & Photographs Division, Library of Congress, LC-USZC4-7824. **26** gary milner/ iStockphoto. **27** (bg) Angela Cable/iStockphoto. (t) The Granger Collection, New York. **28** (bg) Angela Cable/iStockphoto. (cl) Jupiterimages. (cr) The Granger Collection, New York. (tl) PhotoDisc/Getty Images. **29** (bl) Michael S. Quinton/National Geographic Image Collection. (cr) Liz Garza Williams/Hampton-Brown/National Geographic School Publishing.

Illustrator Credits
30-31 Peter Grosshauser

National Geographic School Publishing
Hampton-Brown
www.NGSP.com

Printed in the USA.
Quad Graphics, Leominster, MA

ISBN:978-0-7362-8087-7

17 18 19
10 9 8 7 6